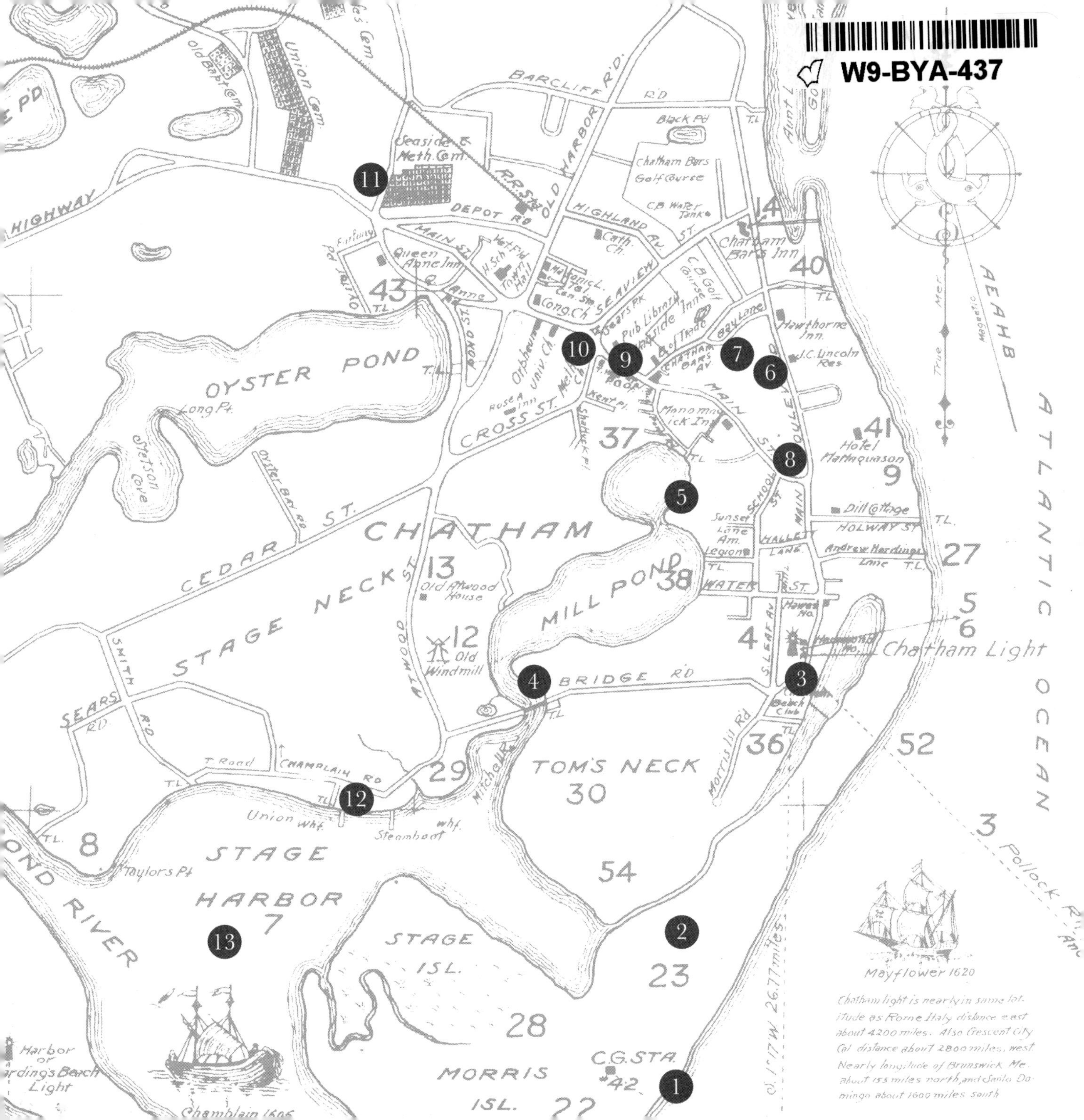

CHATHAM
ATLANTIC OCEAN
OYSTER POND
MILL POND
STAGE NECK
STAGE HARBOR
STAGE ISL.
TOM'S NECK
MORRIS ISL.
OYSTER POND RIVER
HIGHWAY
BARCLIFF R'D.
OLD HARBOR R'D.
DEPOT RD
MAIN ST.
HIGHLAND AV.
SEAVIEW ST.
CROSS ST.
CEDAR ST.
BRIDGE RD
CHAMPLAIN RD
SEARS RD.
SMITH R.D
ATWOOD ST.
HOLWAY ST.
HALLETT LANE
WATER ST.
SCHOOL ST.
Bay Lane
Andrew Harding Lane
Chatham Bars Golf Course
Chatham Bars Inn
Black Pd
CB Water Tank
Seaside & Meth. Cem.
Union Cem.
Old Bapt. Cem.
Queen Anne Inn
Cath. Ch.
Cong. Ch
Pub Library
Sears Pk.
Hawthorne Inn.
J.C. Lincoln Res
Hotel Mattaquason
Dill Cottage
Monomoy ick Inn
Sunset Lane
Am. Legion
Old Atwood House
Old Windmill
Chatham Light
Beach Club
Morris Isl. Rd
Union Whf.
Steamboat whf.
Taylors Pt
Long Pt.
Stetson Cove
C.G. STA.
Pollock R.
Mayflower 1620
Champlain 1606
Harbor or Harding's Beach Light
Chatham light is nearly in same latitude as Rome Italy distance east about 4200 miles. Also Crescent City Cal. distance about 2800 miles west. Nearly longitude of Brunswick Me. about 155 miles north, and Santo Domingo about 1600 miles south
1
2
3
4
5
6
7
8
9
10
11
12
13

THE ORB OF CHATHAM

Bob Staake

COMMONWEALTH EDITIONS

Beverly, Massachusetts

If the characters in this book bear any resemblance to actual persons, living or dead, it is purely coincidental.

ISBN-13: 978-1-933212-14-2
ISBN-10: 1-933212-14-4

Library of Congress Cataloging-in-Publication Data
Staake, Bob, 1957–
  The Orb of Chatham / Bob Staake.
     p. cm.
  ISBN 1-933212-14-4
  1. Unidentified flying objects—Sightings and encounters—Massachusetts—Chatham.
I. Title.
  TL789.5.M4S73 2005
  001.942'09744'92—dc22   2005008637

Design by Bob Staake (BobStaake.com). The font is Baskerville, and the paper is Jenson Satin. Printed in Canada by Friesens.

Commonwealth Editions
266 Cabot Street, Beverly, Massachusetts 01915
www.commonwealtheditions.com

First printing

On a late summer night in 1935, five residents of Chatham, Massachusetts, witnessed a large mysterious "Orb" moving through the small fishing village on the elbow of Cape Cod.

Phone service was uncommon in isolated areas at the time, so the witnesses filed their reports after daylight. Local authorities immediately dismissed them as a hoax.

The witnesses' independent accounts were virtually identical: the Orb appeared to be made of blackened metal, it was perhaps six feet tall, and it traveled in absolute silence by rolling or floating. One witness reported spotting the Orb "hovering" in the air above a local church.

Two months later, all five witnesses vanished on the same October evening—never to be seen again.

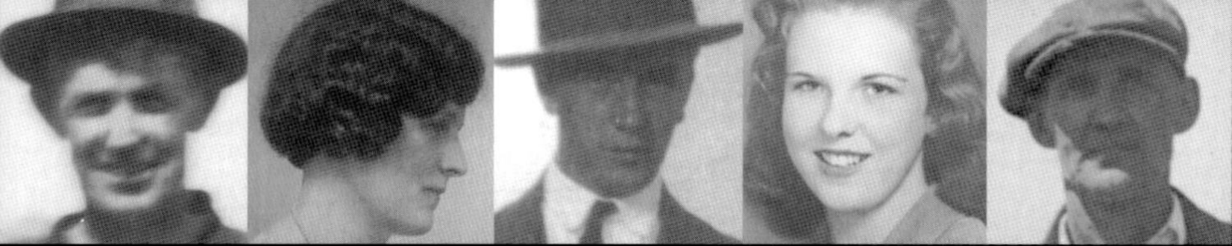

rrived in utter quiet, its perfect shape
ouetted between the sand and the mod

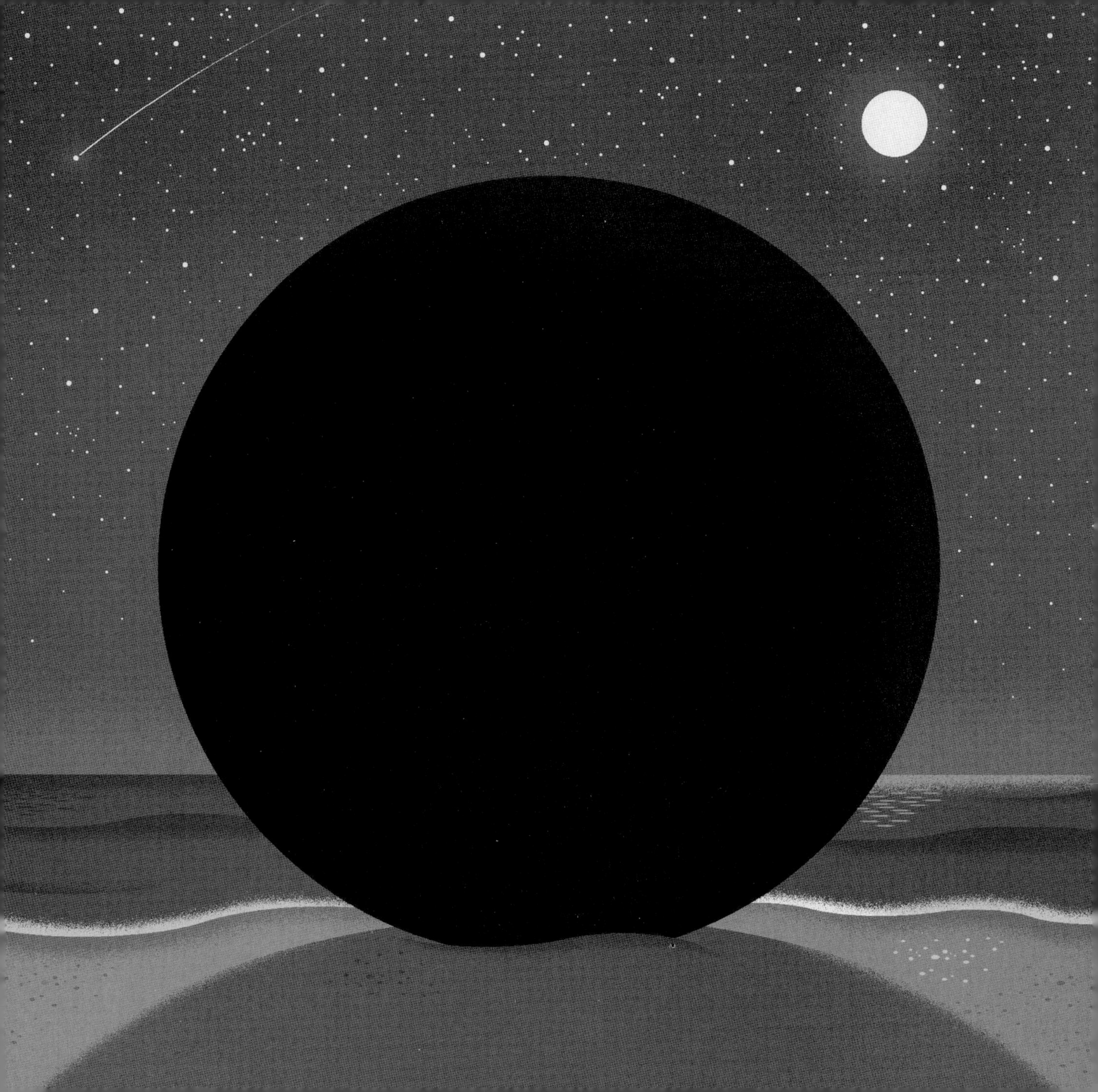

Rolling over the dunes and across
the beach grass, it traveled purposefully.

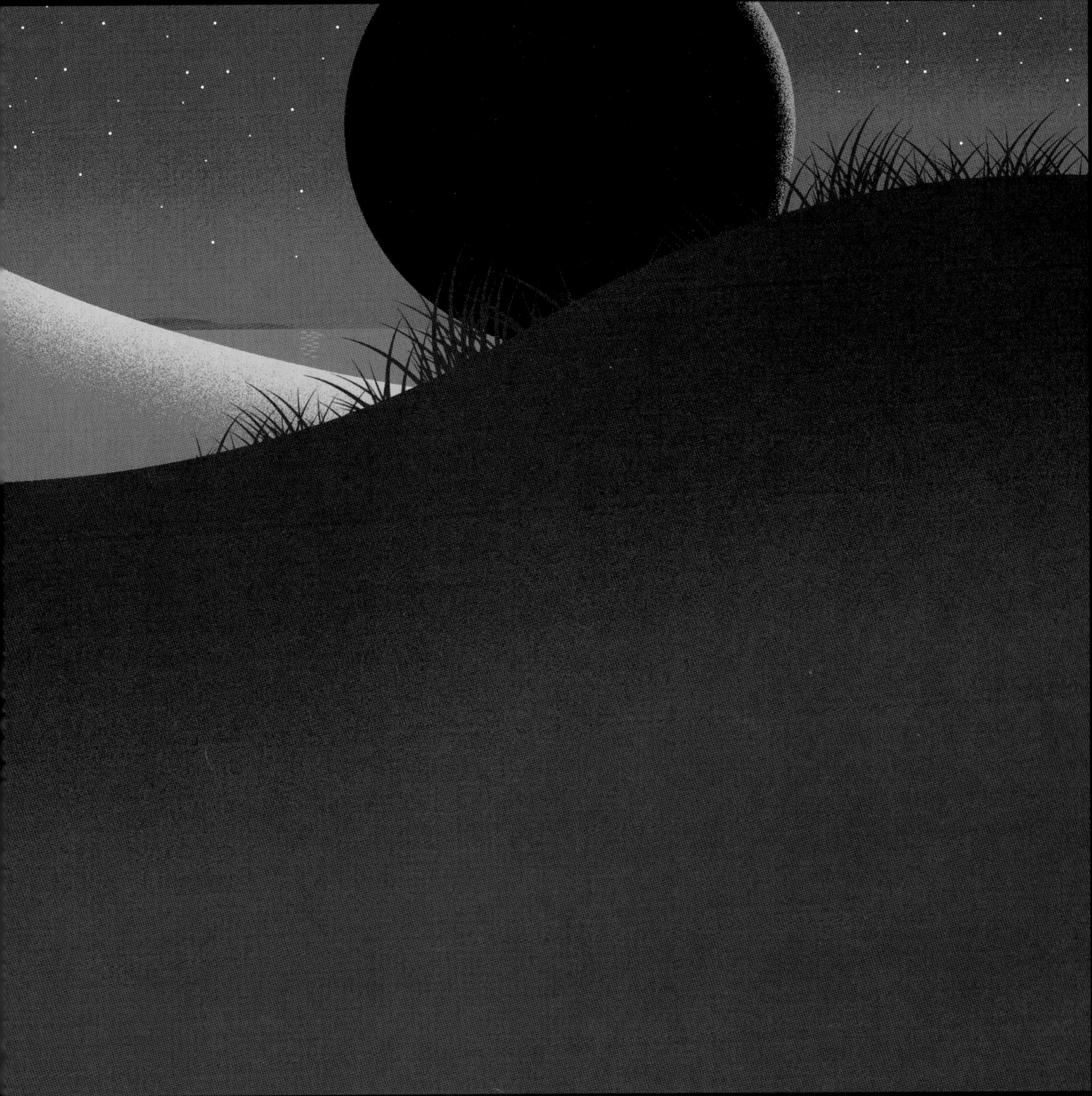

It timed its journey to avoid the light.

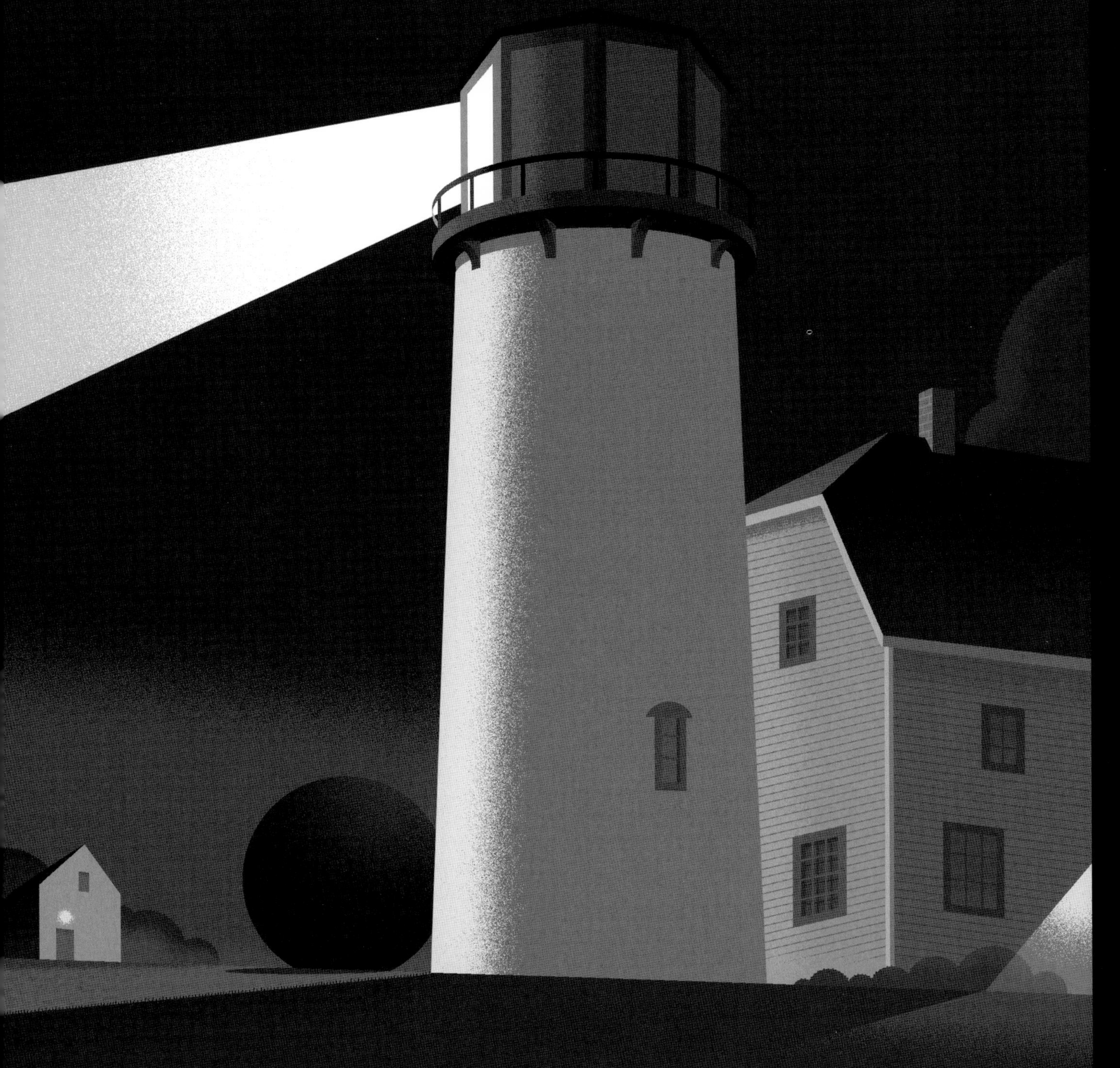

Floating when necessary, it took its cues from the Atlantic tide but kept low when passersby appeared.

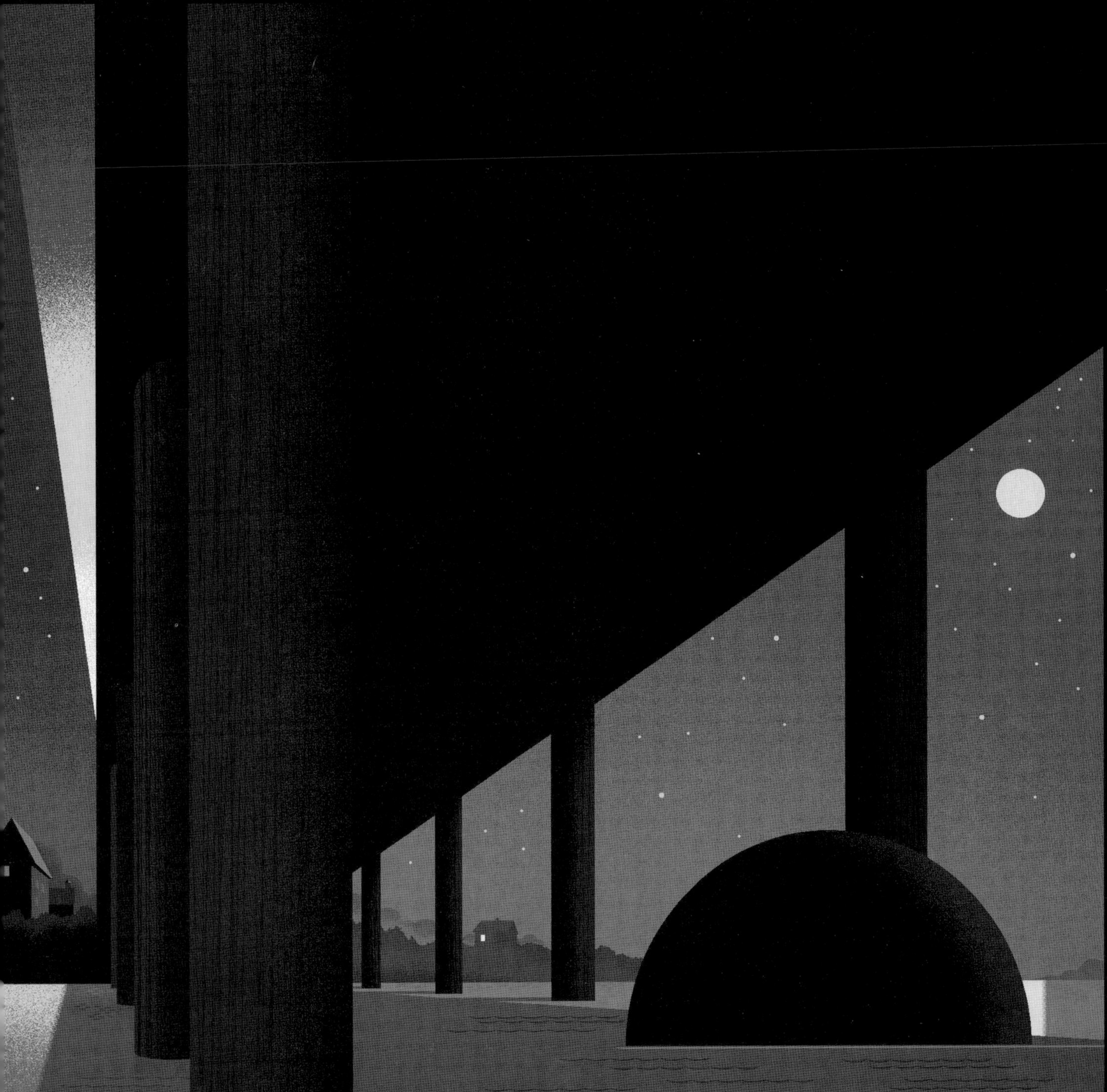

It followed the well-trod path along the salt marsh.

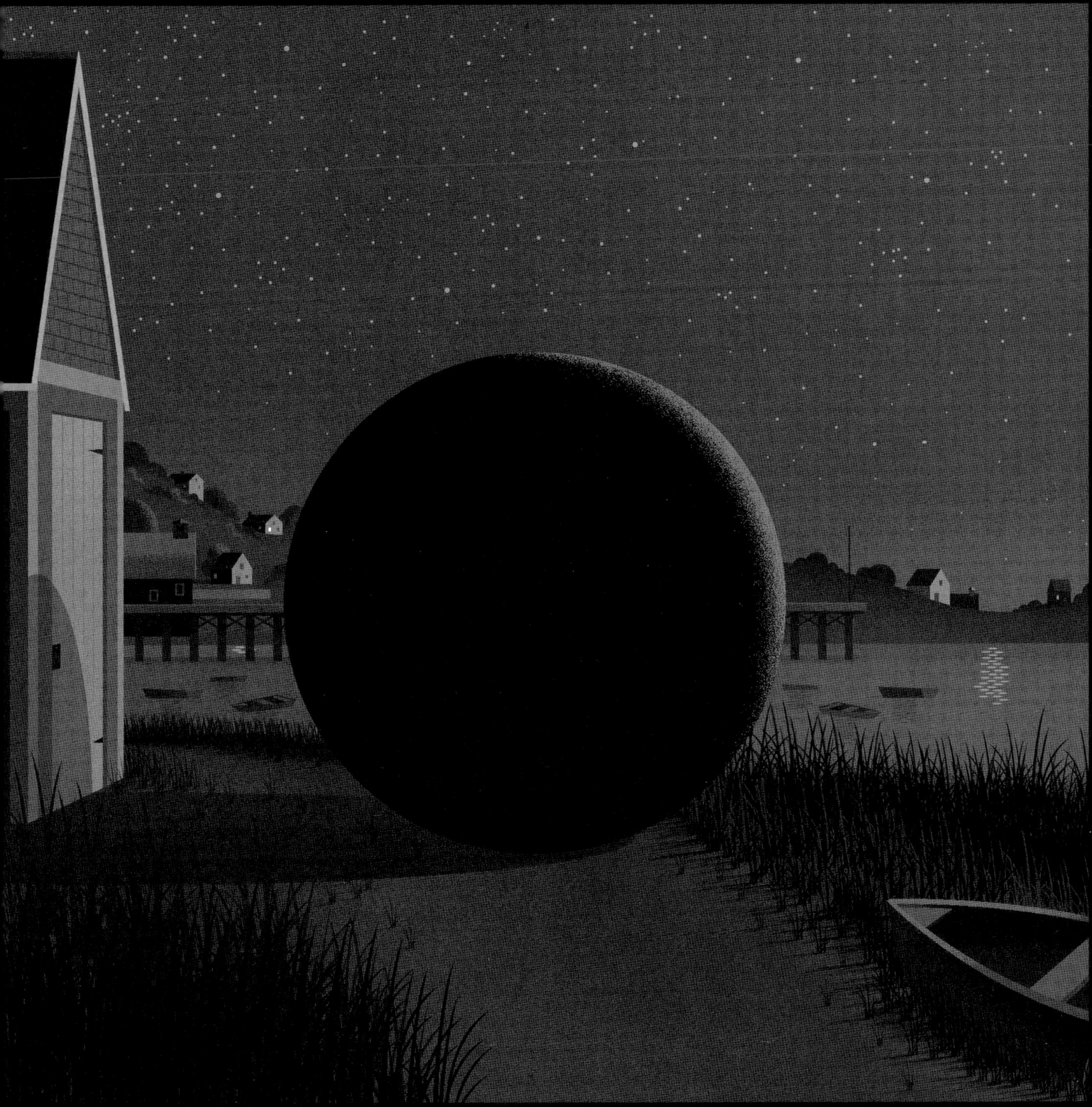

The hills of Shore Road were no obstacle,

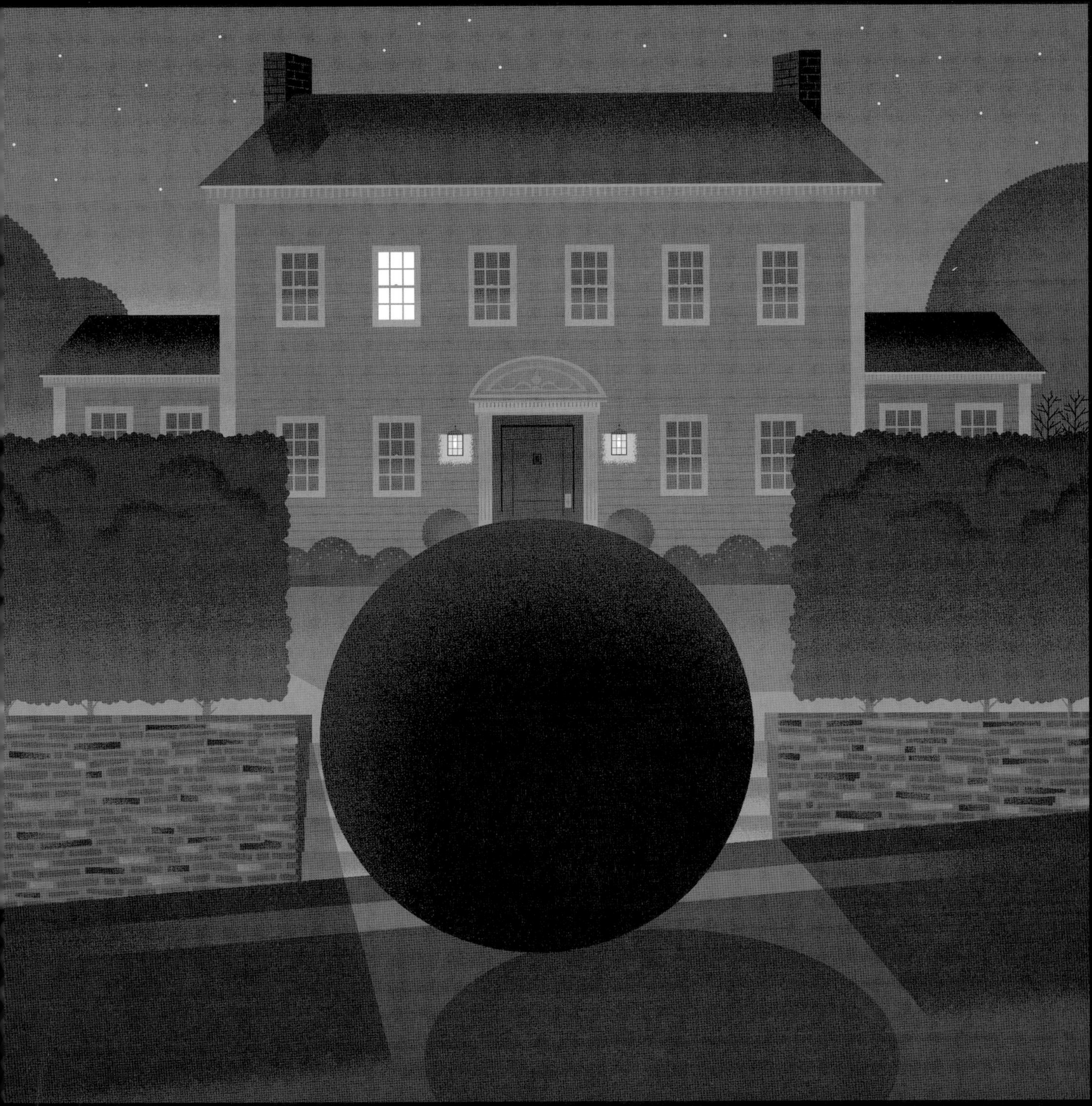

although it entered only one home,
a stately mansion with commanding
views of the Atlantic.

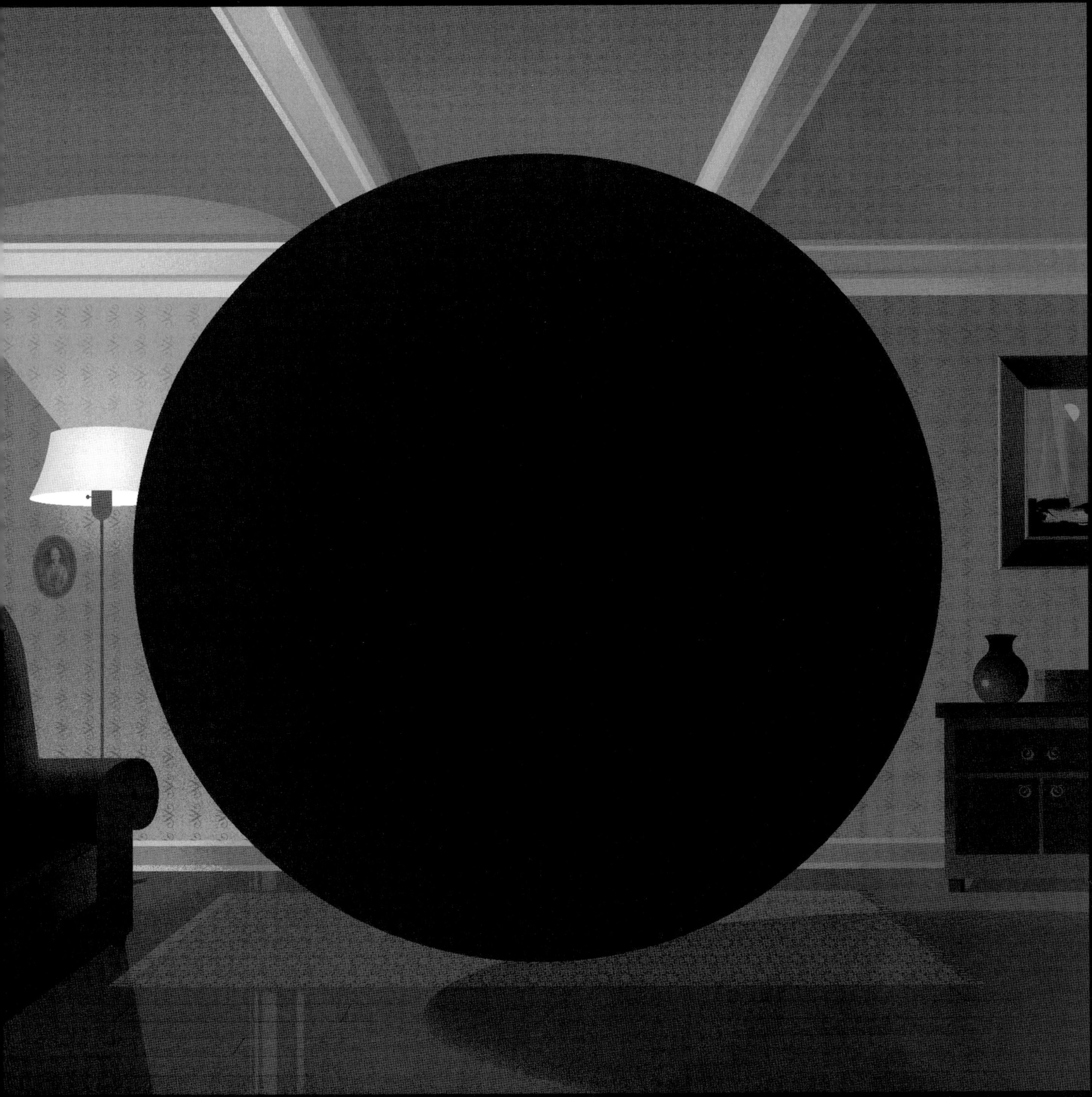

Down Main Street it moved eerily
in complete silence,

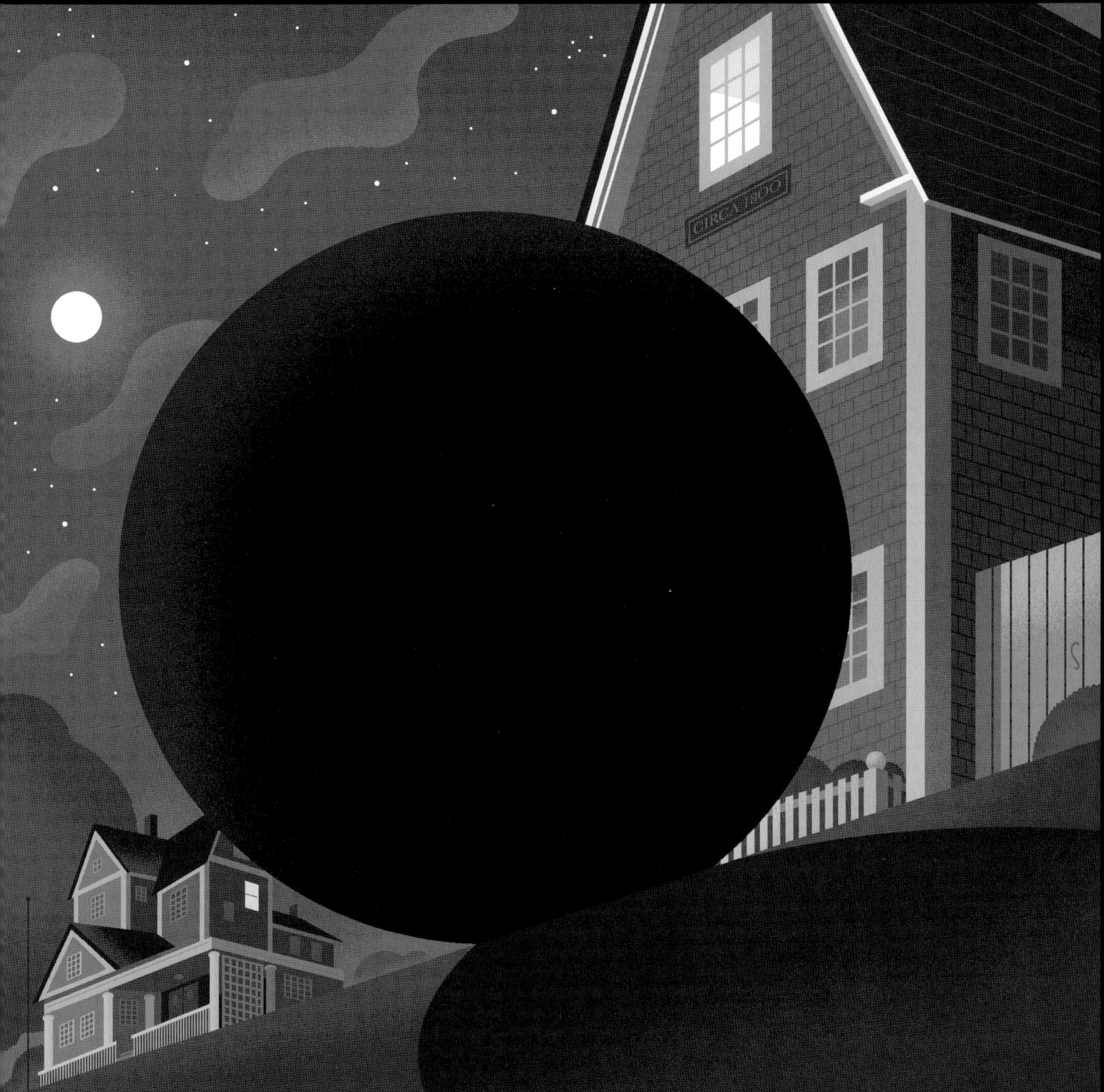
CIRCA 1800

yet it could levitate if need be.

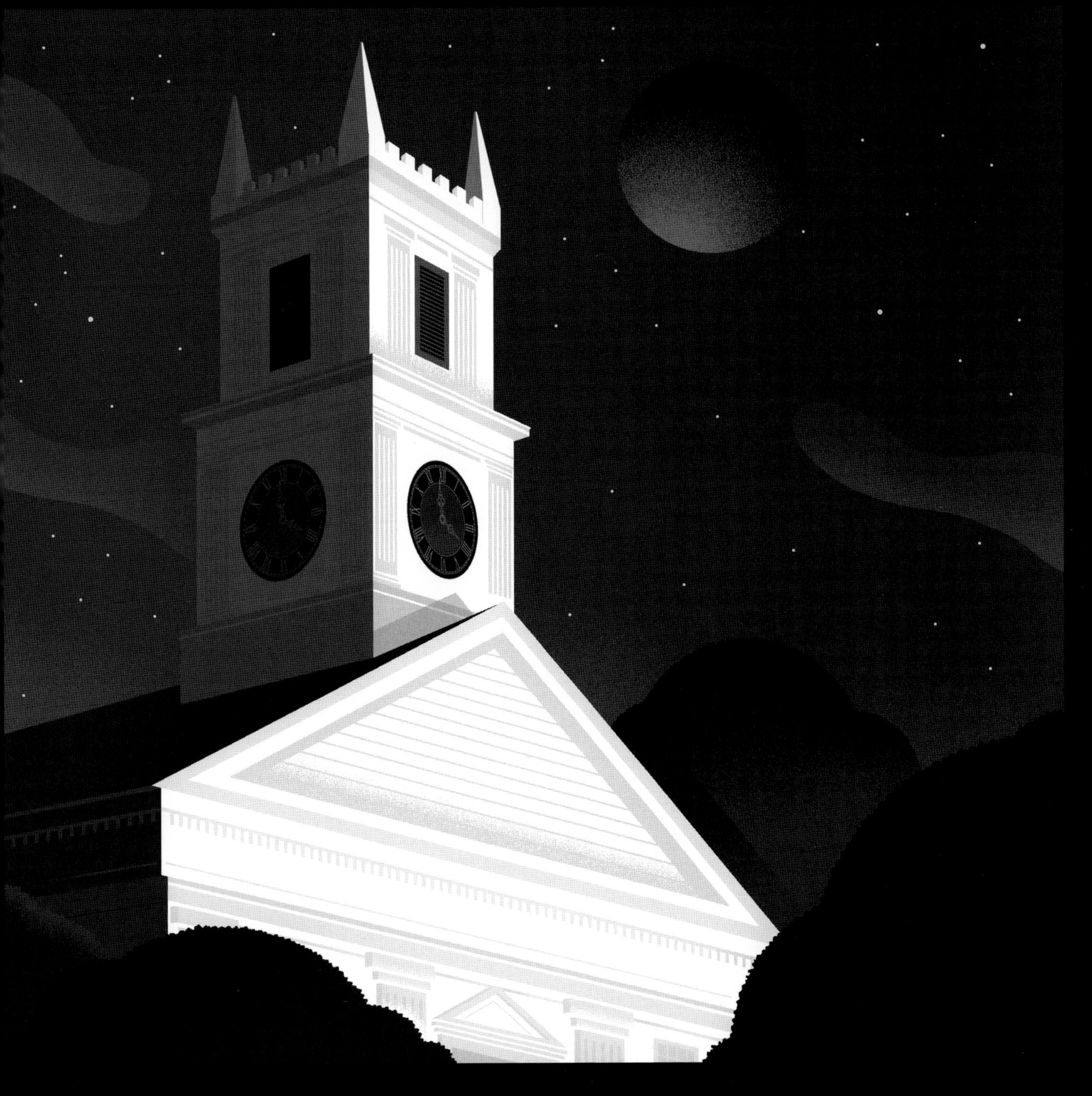

When a room at the inn went bright, it halted. When it sensed that it was safe, it began to roll again, but this time it did so with an almost human aura of caution.

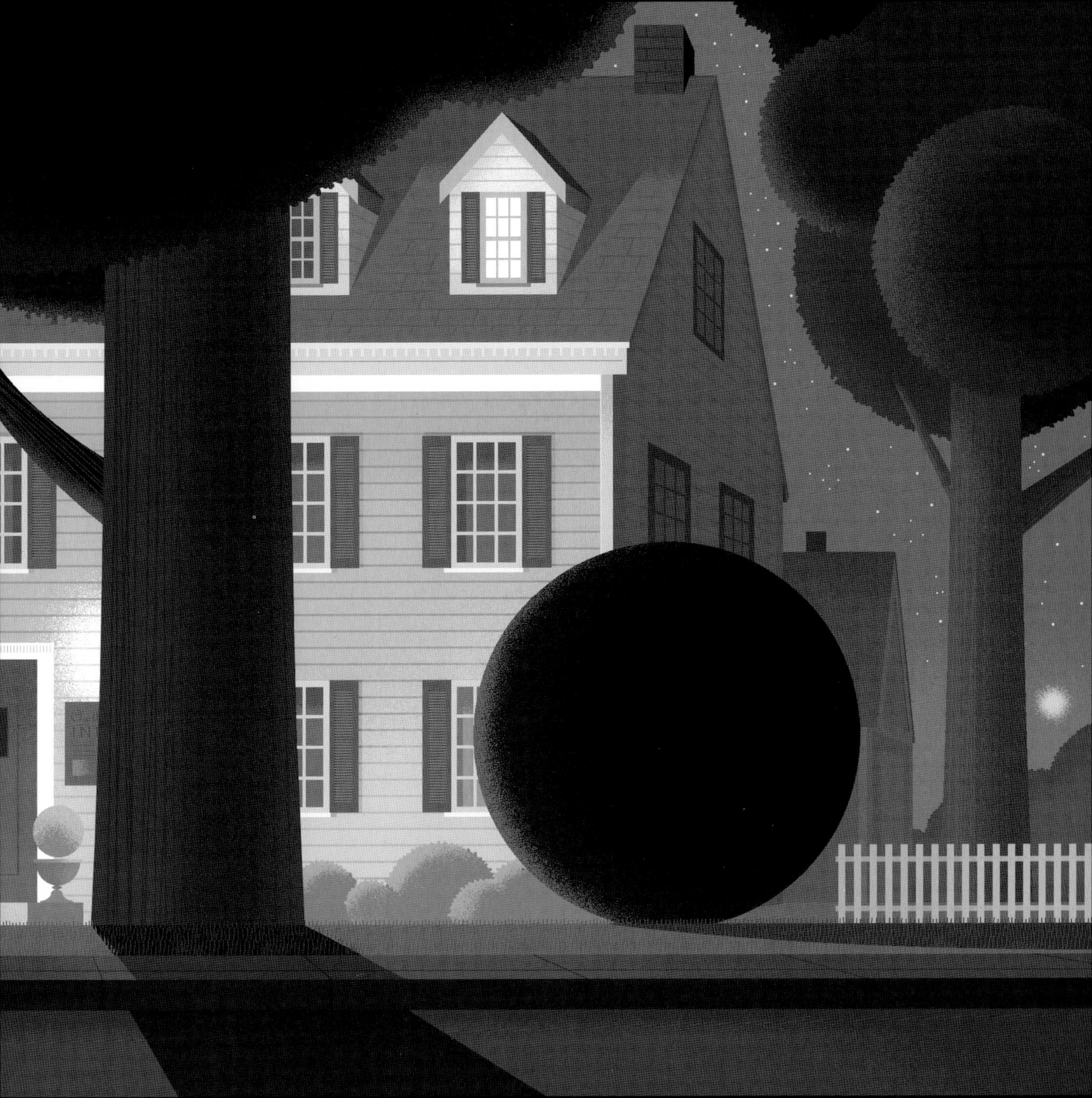

Carefully it meandered amidst the weathered gravestones in Seaside Cemetery.

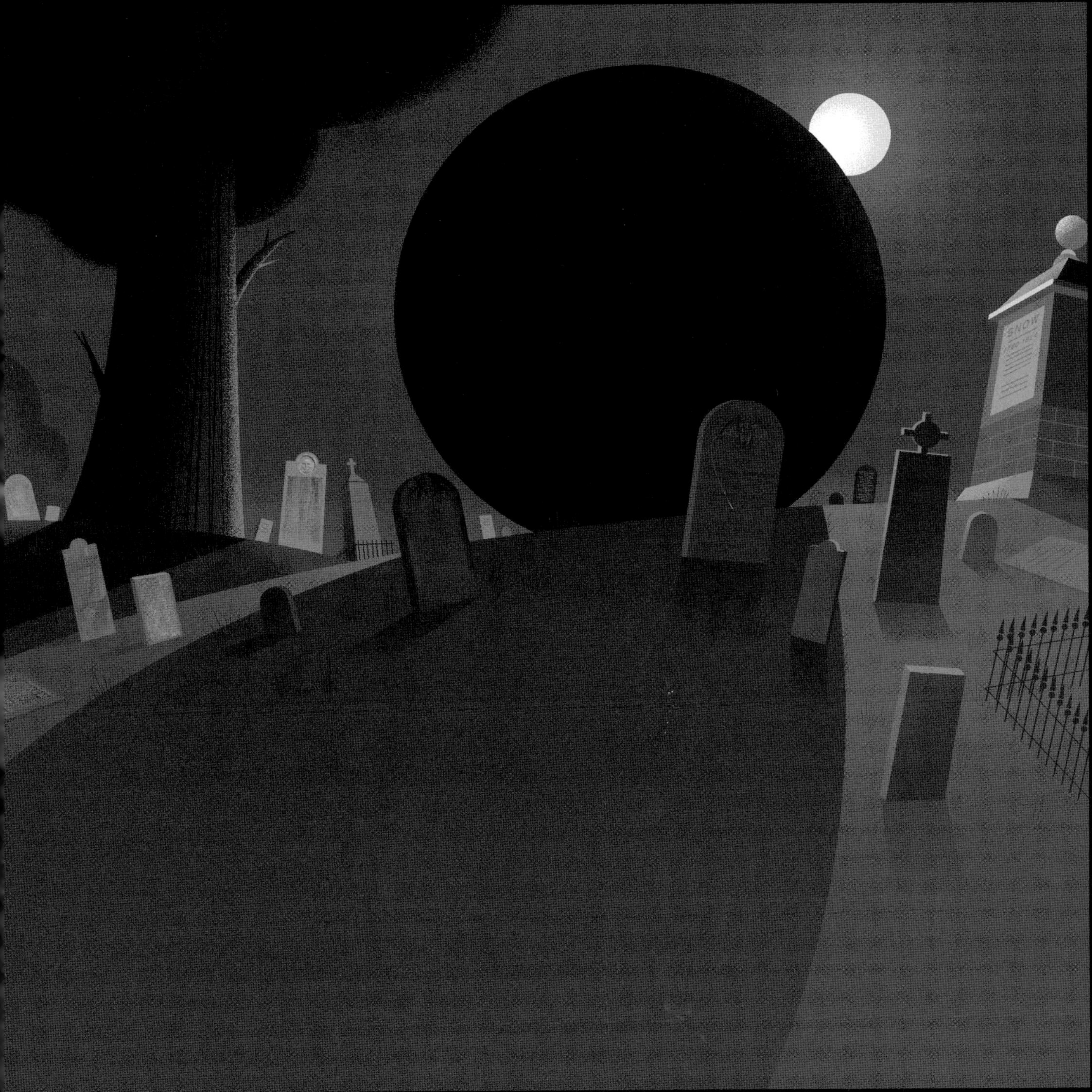
SNOW

It was last seen pushing through the
fog that hung heavy at Stage Harbor.

But where the Orb lies hidden today
beneath the waters of Chatham
remains a mystery.

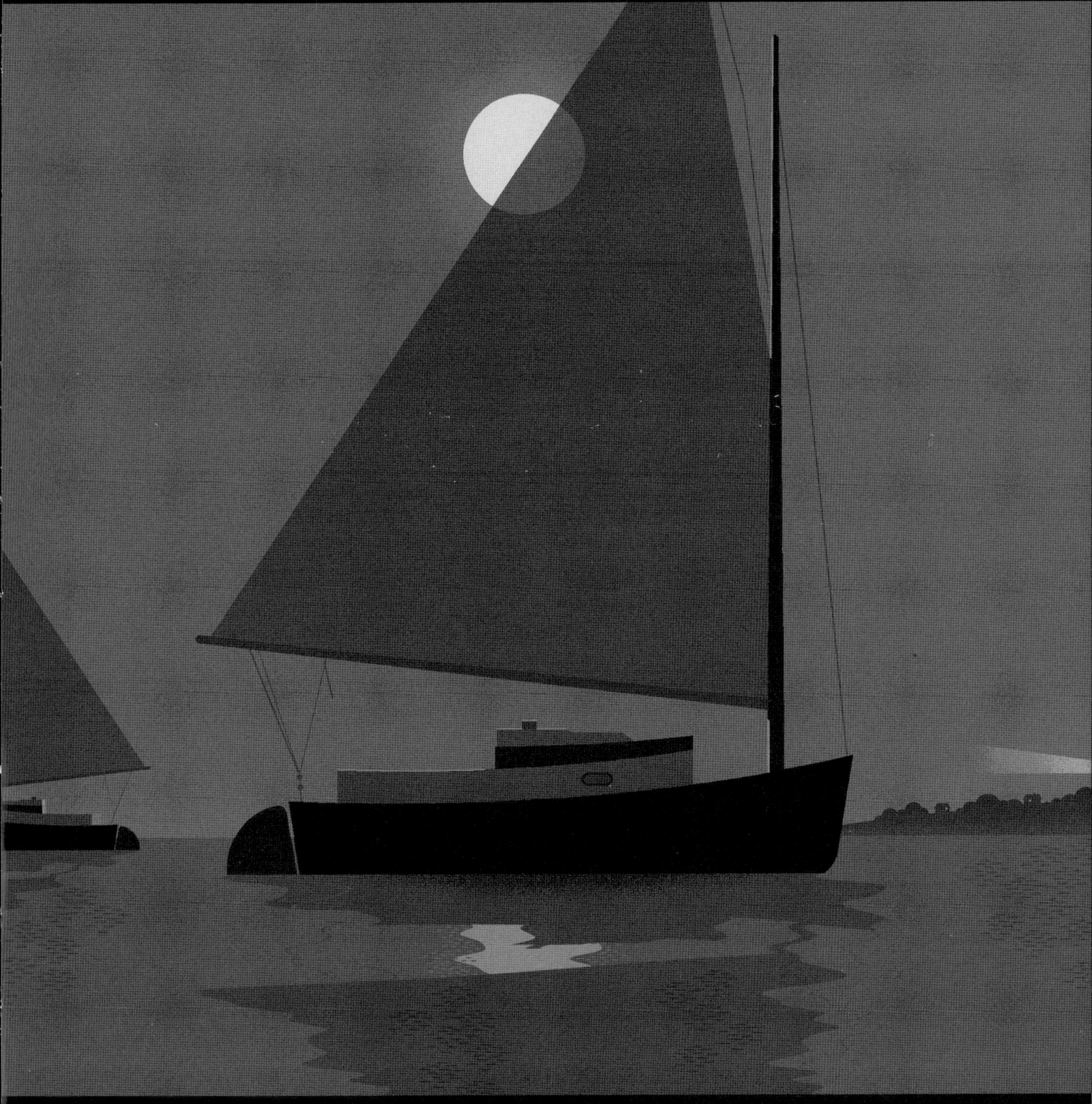

Within this book's artwork lies
a hidden code.

Solving it enables you to
unlock the secret behind
the "Orb of Chatham."

Please visit OrbOfChatham.com.

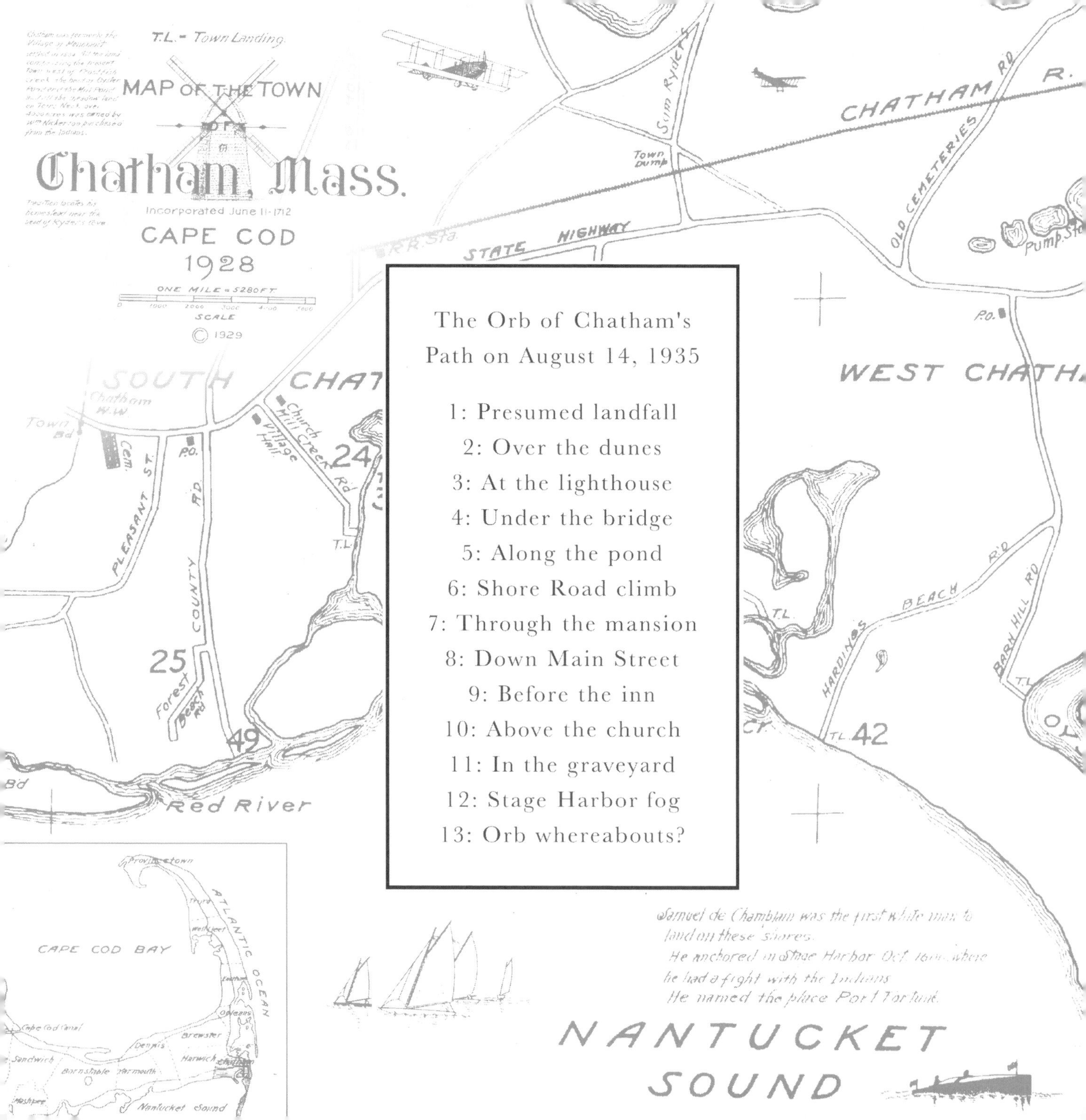

T.L. - Town Landing
MAP OF THE TOWN OF
Chatham, Mass.
Incorporated June 11-1712
CAPE COD
1928
ONE MILE = 5280 FT.
SCALE
© 1929
CHATHAM
R.
Sam Ryders
Town Dump
OLD CEMETERIES
Pump Sta.
R.R. Sta.
STATE HIGHWAY
P.O.
SOUTH
CHAT
WEST CHATH
Town Rd
Cem.
PLEASANT ST.
COUNTY RD.
P.O.
Village Hall
Church
Mill Creek
Rd
24
T.L.
25
Forest
Beach Rd
49
Red River
T.L.
BEACH RD
HARDINGS
BARN HILL RD
T.L.
T.L. 42
Cr.
CAPE COD BAY
ATLANTIC OCEAN
Provincetown
Truro
Wellfleet
Eastham
Orleans
Cape Cod Canal
Brewster
Dennis
Sandwich
Barnstable
Yarmouth
Harwich
Chatham
Mashpee
Nantucket Sound
Samuel de Champlain was the first white man to
land on these shores.
He anchored in Stage Harbor Oct. 1606 where
he had a fight with the Indians.
He named the place Port Fortune.
NANTUCKET
SOUND

The Orb of Chatham's
Path on August 14, 1935

1: Presumed landfall
2: Over the dunes
3: At the lighthouse
4: Under the bridge
5: Along the pond
6: Shore Road climb
7: Through the mansion
8: Down Main Street
9: Before the inn
10: Above the church
11: In the graveyard
12: Stage Harbor fog
13: Orb whereabouts?